# Maui Travel Guide

*Experience the Best Places
to Stay, Eat, Drink, Hike,
Bike, Beach, Surf, Snorkel,
and Discover
in Maui Hawaii*

by Jonathan Saito

# Table of Contents

# Introduction

Legend has it that the Hawaiian Islands were discovered by Hawai'iloa, a Polynesian navigator who named each of the major islands after his sons. Maui was one of them. But, the son, himself was named after the Polynesian demigod, Maui. The latter was responsible for creating the island chain, slowing the sun's path across the sky, and raising the sky's height so people didn't have to stoop so low.

According to geologists who lack such imagination, however, the island was formed from the lava flow of the two volcanic chains to the northwest and southeast, which still dominate the island today. The lava they produced met and formed the rest of Maui. Because of this, Maui is the second biggest land mass in the Hawaiian island chain and officially called the "Valley Isle" due to its many valleys and the vast isthmus between the two volcanic chains.

Originally, Maui was called Ihikapalaumaewa, but fortunately they've shortened it (I wonder why?). To those who call it home, however, well… they simply refer to it as "The Best," and with good reason, too.

Technically speaking, Maui is not a single island, but part of several others which include Lana'i,

Kaho'olawe, Moloka'i, and Penguin Bank (now underwater). Because the channels which separate them are not very deep, they were actually once a single island some 20,000 years ago when sea levels were lower. Administratively, however, those other islands are officially part of what's called the Maui Nui.

There are no big cities in Maui. Everyone lives in small towns, the biggest being Kahului, which hosts the main airport and is the island's commercial hub. The biggest draw, however, is the smaller town of Lahaina, once the capital of the former Kingdom of Hawaii. While it's no longer the capital of anything, it is still crammed with historic colonial architecture and is considered a leading art center.

Right beside this artsy town is Lahaina Harbor, once the playground of Hawaiian nobility. You won't find spectacular enormous waves breaking here, only gentle ones which provide the ideal location for beginners to learn the ancient sport of the former Hawaiian kings: Surfing.

Though largely tropical, Maui's climate varies depending on which side of the island you're on, and how high up or how low down you are. Due to its mountains and valleys, there are many microclimates throughout—from the downright tropical and humid

2

to the arid and desert-like, all the way to colder mountainous regions complete with snow.

Maui is not a heavily industrialized area, which is exactly the way most people like it. People go to the island to enjoy nature, but that doesn't mean it doesn't offer something for everyone. Whether you're a nature freak, a surfing buff, a culture vulture in search of historical tidbits, or the more cosmopolitan type who's into shopping or sophisticated nightlife, Maui definitely has plenty to offer!

# Chapter 1: Best Times to Go

There is no single *best* time to visit Maui. It all depends on what you're after, and equally important, what your budget is.

Keep track of the weather reports, however, especially during **hurricane season**, which runs from August till the end of November. While some hurricanes occur as early as June, August to September is when they peak. By October, hurricanes decline, and by November, they become even rarer.

**December to March** is the major tourist season, but despite being winter in the Northern hemisphere, the island is tropical. This means that the temperature in the lowlands stays in the 80's. If swimming is your thing, this isn't a great time to visit as the waves become too rough, but if you're into surfing, this is the perfect season. If you're into whale watching, this is definitely the best time to visit.

Since this is the tourist season, however, prices of travel and accommodation soar, as do the cost of those trinkets and souvenirs, so consider yourself warned. The two major events at this time are Hyundai's Tournament of Champions PGA (that's golf, by the way) which takes place in January, and the

Maui Chinese New Year Festival which is either February or March (depending on the lunar calendar).

**April to May** is the best time to vacation. The temperature still stays in the 80's, but the tourists have mostly gone, which means you can get great deals on travel and lodging. You can also avoid the hassles of lines and long waiting periods for everything. And since the hoards have left, also expect great deals on those trinkets.

Major events during this period are the East Maui Taro (a vegetable staple) Festival and the Maui Steel Guitar Festival in April, as well as the Maui Onion Festival in May. This is also Golden Week in Japan, a series of national holidays that starts on April 29 and ends on May 5, so expect a lot of Japanese-speaking tourists throughout the islands.

**June to August** is summer season, which is when the hoards return. This means that prices go through the roof, yet again, and reservations are a definite must unless you like the idea of camping out on the beach.

Major events include the Hawaiian Slack-key Guitar Festival, the Kapalua Wine & Food Festival, and the Maui Film Festival in June, as well as the Hawaii State Windsurfing Championship in August.

**September to November** - barring the hurricanes - is another great time to visit, as the more moneyed ones leave. Weather-wise, it's neither too hot nor too cold, except at the mountain peaks where it remains snow-capped the whole year through. Swimmers are advised to stay away from most beaches, as the tides have returned, making it a surfer's paradise... except when the hurricanes come in, of course.

# Chapter 2: Getting to Know the Micro-Climates

Most people don't understand micro-climates, so this requires a chapter of its own. While casual wear (sandals, shorts, and t-shirts) is the norm throughout most of Maui (except for formal occasions), where you are, also plays a role in what you wear, what to expect, and what you can do.

There are six major micro-climates on the island, but since much of it remains either uninhabited or sparsely so, we'll focus on the four which affects most of its residents.

- **Central Maui** refers to Wailuku and Kahului. The latter lies at the island's center and enjoys high temperatures the whole year through. This area experiences dry, desert-like conditions relieved by frequent breezes, and can be uncomfortably muggy at times.

- **Leeward Side** covers South Maui (Kihei, Wailea, and Makena) and West Maui (Lahaina, Kaanapali, and Kapalua), which are even drier than Central with less rain.

11

Average daytime temperatures go as high as 92°. The West Maui summit is unpopulated but open to hikers, and enjoys plenty of rain on its northern and eastern sides. Because of heavy rainfall, the area is sometimes closed off for safety reasons due to landslides.

- **Windward Side** spans the North Shore (Paia and Haiku) and East Maui (Keanae, Hana, and Kipahulu). It rains a lot here, and as its name suggests, is also windier and cooler, which intensifies the higher up you go.

Beaches in these areas are not generally ideal for swimming and snorkeling, but are a surfer's paradise due to the high waves. It all depends on the season, of course. Summer sees calmer seas, making it ideal for swimming, but less so for surfing.

- **Upcountry Maui** includes Makawao, Pukalani, and Kula. This is home to ranches, farms, and botanical gardens, which provide some of the island's freshest produce. Located at 1,700 to 4,500 feet, days and nights are cool. Upper

Kula enjoys morning temperatures as low as 40°, while the Haleakala summit can fall below freezing. Definitely not for shorts, sandals, and t-shirts.

Kona Storms are seasonal cyclones that occur during the winter season striking the southern and western portions. They hit from the west (the leeward side), bringing heavy rain, hail, flash floods, and landslides. In the upcountry, they also bring snow.

When visiting Maui, therefore, take the season and the region into consideration when planning your itinerary. Doing so can save you a lot of hassle and disappointment.

# Chapter 3: Traveling to Maui from the US Mainland

The first thing you should know is that much of what's available on the Hawaiian Islands is generally more expensive than in the U.S. This is because a lot of what they have throughout Hawaii is imported. Some things, like locally grown food, is indeed cheaper, but much of everything else, including fuel, has to be shipped or flown in.

That said, it's generally cheaper to get to Maui from the West Coast than it is from the East Coast, obviously because it's closer. If you're flying from San Francisco, ticket prices vary from $350 to $650, depending on the season and deals available. You can get flights from Los Angeles for about $50 less, again depending on the season, while those flying from the West Coast can expect to pay about $50 more.

The other thing you have to consider is which airport to land at. One option is making your way to Honolulu and from there, to Maui via boat or plane. A more direct option is to fly directly into Maui and land at any of its three airports.

The bigger carriers land at the Kahului Airport (airport code OGG) east of Kahului city. About 99% of domestic and international flights land at Kahului. This is a great idea, since the airport provides full service options, including car rentals and tours.

Kapalua Airport (JHM) only handles commuter types, as well as the smaller prop planes, but it is also accessible from the mainland.

Hana Airport is on the east shore and largely for commuter planes that fly the inter-island routes. With inter-island air routes costing about $200 one way, this is not the best option if you're on a tight budget. Hana is quite far from most of the tourist spots, and driving to and from it can take as long as three hours one way. If you have a lot of time, that might not be a problem, but unless you're coming from some other island, it's not advisable.

If your time is limited and you want to do the Road to Hana spiel (where you can visit the world famous Whaler's Resort), then flying into the Hana Airport might just be what you need. Pacific Wings is the major carrier that serves this small facility.

To save time and money, just do what most do by entering and leaving Maui via Kahului and Kapalua.

Daily ferry services are also available from Lanai and Molokai to Maui.

While a number of online sites claim to offer great deals, nothing beats travel agents. Since they compete with each other by buying blocks (that's group seats sold at discounted rates for bulk purchases), they often provide better deals with more flexible travel options, often with a lot of bells and whistles thrown in.

If you time things right and do your research, flying to Maui from the U.S. can actually make up a smaller portion of your travel expenses. Again, however, it all depends on your itinerary, your tastes, and of course, your budget.

# Chapter 4: The Best Budget Accommodations

If money were no object to you, then you wouldn't be reading this, right? The fact that you are reading it suggests that like the vast majority, money is something you work hard for and have to budget accordingly.

The following rate highly, based on their price range and amenities, according to fellow travelers. This usually (but not always) means no frills, but clean, usually well-located, and with decent to good service. Bear in mind that prices vary depending on the season, but usually hover near the $100 range per night throughout the year.

Hana Kai Maui in Hana is not actually a hotel, but a condominium whose units are each maintained by different management companies. It's at the end of a long twisty road which ends on a black sand beach in a quiet location. Despite this, it's near several restaurants and the Hasegawa General Store, so you can stock up. Many units also sport their own kitchens, so you can save by cooking in your own quarters. Sculpted gardens around the property complete this idyllic getaway.
(http://www.hanakaimaui.com/)

<u>Maui Beach Hotel</u> in Kahului is more of a budget motel in the city, close to the airport, shops, restaurants, and night life. Though close to the beach, it also has its own on-site swimming pool. Note, however, that as of May 2015, the hotel is undergoing renovations and upgrades, so expect a lot of noise and unavailable rooms.
(http://www.mauibeachhotel.net/)

<u>Maui Seaside Hotel</u> is within the town of Kahului, about five minutes' drive from the airport. Located next to the beach and right beside the canoe club, it also sports a modest pool. Best of all, there are plenty of shopping and dining options available nearby. If you'd rather not leave, they have an on-site restaurant which locals visit.
(http://www.mauiseasidehotel.com/)

<u>Maui Sunseeker LGBT Resort</u> in Kihei is for members of the Rainbow Nation. If that still doesn't ring a bell with you, LGBT stands for lesbian, gay, bi, and transgender. That said, you don't actually have to be one to stay there as it's open to everyone... so long as you're adults, that is.

The place offers a variety of apartments from studios to penthouses, all with kitchens. The beach is right across the street, though they have their own on-site salt water pool, hot tub, and landscaped garden

complete with waterfall and rooftop deck for sunbathing.
(http://mauisunseeker.com/)

Aina Nalu in Lahaina is part of the Outrigger Resorts chain, so it consistently gets great reviews because of its great service, cleanliness, and central location. Located just a block away from the main street, you're right near the restaurants and shops, but can also cook in the in-room kitchens. It also boasts two pools on site, as well as a restaurant.
(http://www.outrigger.com/hotels-resorts/hawaiian-islands/maui/outrigger-aina-nalu/overview?CID=PBL-TripAdvisor_Global_Hotel_Website_Link_OAN_20150430_)

Aston at Papakea Resort in Lahaina boasts two pools, a good thing, too. Though right next to the beach, swimming is forbidden during some seasons due to the strong currents. The gardens are well-maintained, while the views are to die for. Not an upscale place, but it provides great value for the price.
(http://www.astonatpapakea.com/?utm_source=tripadvisor&utm_medium=bl-link&utm_campaign=ta-website)

Aston Maui Kaanapai Villas in Lahaina is a bit lower end and further from the beach, but is a walking distance from it. As usual, it boasts a large pool.

Equally important, it's one of the cheaper options in Lahaina.
(http://www.astonmauikaanapalivillas.com/?utm_so
urce=tripadvisor&utm_medium=bl-
link&utm_campaign=ta-website )


Best Western Pioneer Inn in Lahaina is a small and quaint historic colonial building right by the harbor with its own pool. It also boasts two establishments, the Pioneer Inn Grill Bar and the Whalers Saloon, if you like your drinks stronger. It's also a walking distance from most of what the town has to offer.
(http://book.bestwestern.com/bestwestern/US/HI/
Lahaina-hotels/BEST-WESTERN-Pioneer-
Inn/Hotel-
Overview.do?iata=00170230&propertyCode=12012&
sob=TRIPHWS&cm_mmc=BL-_-TRIP-_-
TRIPHWS-_-GENERAL)


Kaanapali Beach Hotel in Lahaina is between the beach on one side and the shops and restaurants on the other. They also host an on-site restaurant and offer various water sporting facilities. The sculpted gardens and breathtaking views also make it a favorite for weddings and receptions, but there is a daily parking fee.
(http://www.kbhmaui.com/)


Kaanapali Ocean Inn in Lahaina is near Whaler's Village on a pristine stretch of Kaanapali Beach. This is not a hotel, but a budget lodge, so don't expect

much in terms of amenities. Price-wise, however, it's hard to beat. Location-wise and in terms of the view, it's equally hard to beat. They have an on-site restaurant and offer car rental services so you can explore the nearby sites. You also get to use the much posher Royal Lahaina right next door, without having to pay a lot more for it.
(http://www.kaanapalioceaninn.com/)


Lahaina Inn, again in Lahaina, is a tiny, saloon-like building smack dab in the center of town, so you're right where all the action is. It's a great deal for the price, but you're also further from the beach and it does get a little noisy at night. If partying is your thing, however, then this is just the place for you.
(http://www.lahainainn.com/)


Lahaina Shores Beach Resort in Lahaina offers kitchens in its rooms, which is great since it's not in the heart of town. Since the whole town is small, however, you can actually walk to it within five minutes, so that's not a problem, especially at night if you prefer it quiet. The marina is also right next to it, as is the reef, which makes it ideal for snorkeling.
(https://gc.synxis.com/rez.aspx?template=Hotel&shell=GCF&Hotel=63000&Chain=17019)


Maui Guest House in Lahaina is a small bed and breakfast that's in a quiet location in a residential neighborhood, but as with most things in Lahaina, everything is within walking distance. Besides the small pool, they only have four rooms, allowing them to give guests a very personalized experience. (http://www.mauiguesthouse.com/)


Napili Shores Lahaina is also part of the Outrigger Resort chain, so it's clean, well-maintained, and offers great amenities. Located right next to Napili Bay, which is ideal for whale watching, it also sports its own on-site pool. Rooms also come equipped with kitchens so you can eat in. Nearby is Napili Plaza where you have several shopping and dining options available. The rooms are not air-conditioned, but the ideal location ensures it remains cool the whole year through.
(http://www.outrigger.com/hotels-resorts/hawaiian-islands/maui/outrigger-napili-shores/overview?CID=PBL-TripAdvisor_Global_Hotel_Website_Link_NSR_201 50430_ )


Paia Inn Hotel in Paia is a small boutique hotel right across the street from the Paia Fish Market. Paia is another draw for artists and is famous for its fresh, organic foods, and shops. The *Los Angeles Times* dubbed the Paia Inn Hotel an, "Upscale Stylish Haven," while the *Travel + Leisure* magazine deemed it, "America's most romantic hotel." Its unique rooms and stylish décor complement its spectacular beachside location and sculpted gardens. The hotel offers free coffee and tea in the lobby, and there's a

coffee shop next door, which serves fruit for breakfast every morning.
(http://paiainn.com/)


Sprecks Plantation House in Spreckelsville is just a few minutes' drive out of Paia in a lush tropical garden between Kite Beach and Ko'okipa beach, both known as the Windsurfing Capital of the World. Each unit is unique, has its own kitchen, and some even boast outdoor showers.
(http://www.sprecksplantationhouse.com/)

# Chapter 5: The Best Places to Eat and Drink

Hawaiian cuisine is a blend of local Polynesian fare mixed with American, Chinese, Filipino, Japanese, Korean, and European cuisine (particularly influenced by Spain and Portugal). The result is a unique mish-mash of food that caters to all tastes. The following are among local favorites which many visitors swear by.

Ba-Le Sandwiches & Bakery has four locations in Kahului, Kihei, Lahaina, and Wailuku, as well as ten more throughout the rest of Hawaii. Despite its Eiffel Tower logo, it's actually a unique Vietnamese take on French cuisine with a lot of Thai, Chinese, and local varieties thrown in.
(http://www.balemaui.com/)

Da Kitchen has branches in Kihei and Kahului, as well as another on Oahu. These were the people who cooked at President Obama's election in 1998 and appeared on several TV shows. Their specialty is local fare, while major favorites are their Pulehu Grilled Steak and their BBQ Beef Steaks.
(http://dakitchen.com/)

Local Boys Shave Ice has branches in Kihei and Lahaina. They specialize in 50 ice flavors, but they're also famous for their Maui Roselani ice cream. They've also expanded their menu to include hot dogs, chili and rice, bagels, as well as coffee. (http://www.localboysshaveice.com/)


Lynne's Café in Haiku is owned and operated by Aunty Lynn, who serves up a no-nonsense array of local favorites, which in Hawaii includes Spam. Lynne's Café is a local tradition, especially the one where you can custom order your meal and have it cooked for you on the spot. (https://www.zomato.com/hawaii/lynnes-cafe-haiku)


Geste Shrimp Truck can be found in Kahului Harbor. It is a truck, but one that's received the Best Food Truck award for two consecutive years. They're open from 10.30 am till 5.30 pm or until they run out of food, so it's best to get to them early. (http://www.gesteshrimp.com/)


Local Food in Lahaina is literally a shack at the Anchor Square Shopping Center, but it got the TripAdvisor Certificate of Excellence in 2013. In terms of ambience, don't expect much, but it is a local favorite. (http://www.localfood.tripod.com/)

Grandma's Maui Coffee in Keokea is famous for roasting and blending their own organic coffee since 1918. Besides great food and pastries, they also provide lovely views from their terrace, and are an excellent pit stop on the Road to Hana.
(http://www.grandmascoffee.com/)

Coconut's Fish Café in Kihei was dubbed one of CNN's, "Top 10 Places to Eat Like a Local" for the entire United States. Fish tacos are a favorite, as are their fish burgers and Seafood Caesar Salad.
(http://www.coconutsfishcafe.com/home)

Eskimo Candy Seafood Market & Deli in Kihei got its name because it started out as a wholesale seafood distributor after its owner visited Alaska in 1987. The restaurant was added in 2003 and has since become famous for its crab cakes, fish and chips, and tempura and coconut shrimp.
(http://www.eskimocandy.com/)

Kihei Caffe in Kihei (obviously) is not a typo; they really spell it with two "F"s. It's been voted, by a local magazine, the "Best Breakfast," for six consecutive years for its 40 breakfast choices. Among the most popular is their Southern Style Sausage Gravy and Biscuits, with everything made on site.
(http://kiheicaffe.com/)

<u>Sansei Seafood Restaurant & Sushi Bar</u> in Kapalua and Kihei has been getting rave reviews from various corners, the most notable being the one by *Bon Appetit Magazine* which dubbed it one of "America's Best Sushi Bars." One of their most famous menu items is the Panko Crusted Ahi Sashimi Sushi Roll. (http://www.sanseihawaii.com/)

<u>Ulupaluakua Ranch Store & Grill</u> in Kula is an actual cattle ranch which spans 18,000 acres of land, so the meat is definitely fresh, organic, and with no chemical additives. It's not just beef they serve, however, but also elk and pork. (http://www.ulupalakuaranch.com/)

<u>Aloha Mixed Plate</u> in Lahaina is by the beach and specializes in local fare and great drinks. Their specialties include Coconut Prawns served with pineapple chutney, which goes great with their Mango Lemonade. (http://www.alohamixedplate.com/)

<u>Fish Market</u> is in Lahaina at Honokowai, which specializes in the fresh catch of the day. Typical of Hawaii, they also serve great sushi and fish burgers, which you can either eat on site or take out with you to the beach. (http://fishmarketmaui.com/)

Ono Kau Kau Mixed Plate in Lahaina offers a no-frills menu of Chinese and Hawaiian cuisine on only four tables. A local favorite is the Spam Musubi, but don't let the Japanese sounding name fool you—it's an Asian take on Spam.
(http://www.tripadvisor.com.ph/Restaurant_Review-g60634-d1899587-Reviews-Ono_Kau_Kau_Mixed_Plate-Lahaina_Maui_Hawaii.html)

Ululani's Hawaiian Shave Ice has four locations, two of which are in Lahaina, while the other two are in Kihei and Kahului. They only use 100% pure cane sugar and natural fruit juices in over 50 flavors with local toppings such as shredded coconut and even piña colada.
(http://www.ululanisshaveice.com/)

T. Komoda Store & Bakery Inc. has been an institution in Makawao Town since 1916. They close early because they run out of stuff quickly, so this is another one that requires an early visit.
(http://www.tripadvisor.com.ph/Restaurant_Review-g60635-d820334-Reviews-T_Komoda_Store_Bakery_Incorporated-Makawao_Maui_Hawaii.html)

Kuau Store in Paia is the last stop before hitting the Road to Hana. It's a general store that also serves juices, coffee, breakfast, and salads, as well as plate lunches.
(http://www.kuaustore.com/)

A Saigon Café in Wailuku has won awards for its authentic Vietnamese food, though it also serves local Hawaiian cuisine. Favorites include the Garden Delight Rolls and Saigon Egg Noodle Soup.
(http://www.urbanspoon.com/cities/37-hawaii/restaurants/410012-a-saigon-cafe/menu)

Sam Sato's Noodles & Plate Lunches in Wailuku has been around since 1933 and has been in the same family for three generations. It's become an institution with locals, whose favorites include the Dry Mein, Teriyaki Beef sticks, and Sweet Lima Manju.
(http://www.frommers.com/destinations/maui/restaurants#sthash.AINyIon6.dpbs)

Tasty Crust in Wailuku has been around for 50 years and claims to serve "World Famous Pancakes." Besides pancakes, they also serve a variety of Korean and Chinese dishes.
(http://www.tastycrust.com/)

# Chapter 6: The Best Biking Trails

Maui takes cycling very seriously and if you want to know more, your first stop should be the Maui Bicycling League. This non-profit organization has been very active throughout the island since 1956 and is part of the League of American Bicyclists. Besides encouraging the expansion of cycling trails throughout Maui and encouraging residents to bike to work, they also help new comers find their way around the island on bicycles.
(http://mauibicyclingleague.org/)

Besides urban trails, Maui also has some of the most spectacular routes best explored by bicycle. Whether you want to go it alone or join a group guided tour, a good resource to check out is Maui Cycling Vacations.
(http://www.mauicyclingvacations.com/)

Another option for guided tours is Maui Downhill, one of the oldest downhill companies on the island. Maui Downhill specializes in morning safaris, inclusive of breakfast, to spectacular peaks for equally spectacular views of sunrises. So if you're not a morning person, this might not be for you. As to the downhill part? Well, after the sun finally rises, you begin a more leisurely bike ride back down hill, hence its name.
(http://www.mauidownhill.com/)

Since Maui is made up of spectacular mountains, no visit to the island would be complete without them. To explore them by bicycle, get in touch with Mountain Riders Bike Tours. This is for the more athletic, though children and pregnant women can come along and ride in the accompanying van. (http://www.mountainriders.com/)

For the more adventurous (and far more energetic), there's also the Haleakala Bike Company. Haleakala is also known as the East Maui Volcano because that's where it's at and that's what it is. The name translates into English as *House of the Sun*, because it was at the peak this Maui was able to tame the sun and make it run slower to lengthen the day. You don't actually have to bike up to the peak, if you're not up to it. You can take a bus up *with* your bike then enjoy the ride down *on* it. (http://www.bikemaui.com/)

Whether you get to Maui with your bicycle, need to buy one, rent one, or have one repaired and maintained, be sure to visit South Maui Bicycles. They're a full service bike shop who'll be happy to help you out. (http://www.southmauibicycles.com/)

# Chapter 7: The Best Beaches

As an island, Maui is surrounded by beaches, so there's simply no way to describe them all. The following, however, are the ones that get great raves for what they offer, as well as keep both locals and tourists coming back.

DT Fleming Park in Kapalua is a no-frills beach that was deemed America's Best Beach in 2003. It's great for swimming, surfing, and body boarding. "No frills" means that while they have life guards, phones, toilets, picnic facilities, and a playground for children, they offer no water sports facilities or other such resort stuff. The good news is that it isn't overly developed. In case you're wondering about the name, DT Fleming was the man who introduced the pineapple to West Maui.
(http://www.co.maui.hi.us/facilities/Facility/Details/170)

Kapalua Beach is a crescent-shaped, palm-lined beach beside the Kapalua Resort. Its calm waters make it ideal for swimming, kayaking, and snorkeling. It also has toilets, showers, and lifeguards for your comfort and safety.
(http://www.lonelyplanet.com/usa/hawaii/kapalua-northern-beaches/sights/beaches-islands-waterfronts/kapalua-beach)

Kaanapali Beach is for those who want it all. It stretches some three miles along one of the island's most developed areas, so you get crystal clear waters on one side, and hotels, resorts, restaurants, and shops on the other. Be sure to also visit the Whalers Village shopping center and any of the two golf courses if you're into that sort of thing. They also host a cliff diving ceremony off Black Rock (known locally as the Puu Kekaa) every evening, so if your time's limited, Kaanapali Beach is the place to be. (http://www.gohawaii.com/en/maui/regions-neighborhoods/west-maui/kaanapali-beach/)

Wailea Beach was named America's Best Beach in 1999 and is one of five connected crescent shaped beaches in the resort community of Wailea. The other beaches are Polo Beach, renowned for swimming and snorkeling, and Ulua Beach Park, which is not so ideal for swimming because of the strong currents. There's also Kahoolawe, Lanai, and Molokini, which are great swimming spots. If you're into whales, this is one of the best places on the island to see them, but they only pass by from December to April. (http://www.gohawaii.com/en/maui/regions-neighborhoods/south-maui/wailea/)

Maluaka Beach, also called Makena Beach, is right beside the Makena Beach & Golf Resort. Known for its sand dunes, it's also called Pu'u One (sand hills). Except for the resort, there are also picnic and toilet facilities available, or you can rent beach equipment

from the resort, itself. This is great for swimming closer to the beach, but since the waves get rougher further off, it's also great for surfers.
(http://www.to-hawaii.com/maui/beaches/maluakabeach.php)

Waianapanapa State Park's beach is renowned for its black sands (which you can't take away), but the rough waters, strong currents, and rocky reef make it too dangerous for swimming. There are other options to see and do, however including hiking, camping, and exploring volcanic caves. Fishing and picnicking are allowed, though there are also cabins available on site.
(http://www.hawaiiweb.com/blog/maui/waianapanapa-state-park-maui)

Hamoa Beach always win's Maui's Best Beaches award, probably because it's a no-frills area with little development. Note, however, that there are no lifeguards available, though there are toilets and showers on site. While it's a good place for swimming, it isn't consistently so, but warning signs are always put up when you shouldn't go in. It's generally great for surfers, but they ban it during winter when the waves become too outrageous. The beach is very narrow, but there's plenty of shade because of all the vegetation.
(http://hamoabeach.org/)

# Conclusion

There's obviously far more to Maui than what's just been described. There's culture, nightlife, historical sites, and other famous attractions to see and experience. To do so, you just have to make your way there, since nothing beats the real experience. A good place to get started is with their official website, <u>Visit Maui</u>, which provides a lot more information, as well as visitor's tips to make your stay easier and more enjoyable.

Finally, I'd like to thank you for purchasing this book! If you enjoyed it or found it helpful, I'd greatly appreciate it if you'd take a moment to leave a review on Amazon. Thank you!